Nov. 6, 2007

When Bears

Attack!

Richard Marshall Gaines

Enslow Publishers, Inc.
40 Industrial Road
Box 398
Berkeley Heights, NJ 07922
USA

http://www.enslow.com

When Wild Animals Attack!

Library of Congress Cataloging-in-Publication Data

Gaines, Richard, 1942–
  When bears attack! / by Richard Marshall Gaines. — 1st ed.
      p. cm. — (When wild animals attack!)
  Includes bibliographical references and index.
  ISBN 0-7660-2669-8
  1. Bear attacks—Juvenile literature. I. Title. II. Series.
  QL737.C27G345 2006
  599.78'165—dc22

                                                    2006010907
Printed in the United States of America

10 9 8 7 6 5 4 3 2 1

To Our Readers:
We have done our best to make sure all Internet Addresses in this book were active and appropriate when we went to press. However, the author and the publisher have no control over and assume no liability for the material available on those Internet sites or on other Web sites they may link to. Any comments or suggestions can be sent by e-mail to comments@enslow.com or to the address on the back cover.

Photo Credits: Associated Press, AP, Phillip King, p. 22; Associated Press, Daily Inter Lake, p. 11; Associated Press, The Mining Journal, pp. 3, 27; Corel Stock Photos, pp. 3, 12, 35; Getty Images, p. 26; Getty Images/Aurora, pp. 25, 30; Getty Images/National Geographic, pp. 21, 34, 36, 39; Getty Images/ Stone, p. 1; Getty Images/The Image Bank, p. 14; North Wind Picture Archives/North Wind, p. 32; Photo Researchers, Inc./ Doug Allan, pp. 3, 28; Photo Researchers, Inc./William Ervin, p. 4; Photo Researchers, Inc./Ralph Lee Hopkins, p. 33; Photo Researchers, Inc./Mark Newman, p. 42; Photo Researchers, Inc./ Art Wolfe, p. 15; Photos.com, pp. 3, 6, 9, 16, 40, 44.

Illustration: Kevin Davidson, p. 19

Cover Photos: Getty Images/Stone (front), Corel Stock Photos (back)

Contents

One

A grizzly bear, photographed in Colorado, shows its aggressive

A Hard Road Back
for a Survivor

In the fall of 1983, a young couple went camping in the wilderness of the Rocky Mountains in Waterton Lakes National Park in Alberta, in western Canada. They hiked to a camping spot on Crypt Lake. When they woke up in their tent the next morning, there was snow on the ground so they hurried to pack up and start back down the trail.

Patricia Van Tighem and her husband, Trevor Janz, had been in bear territory many times before. They knew—or thought they knew—all about bears and how to avoid them. They talked and sang as they went along because park rangers advise people that making noise usually makes bears stay away. Trevor was a little ahead of Patricia, but she could hear him singing. She felt safe.

Then, suddenly, she came around a bend. Just a few feet ahead she saw a grizzly bear charging right at Trevor! It bit him on the leg and he fell to the ground.

Patricia was horrified. What could she do to get the bear off her husband? She remembered park rangers' instructions on what to do in case of a bear attack. She yelled and threw down her pack, hoping to distract the bear, but it did not work. Deep down she knew she could not help. She had to try to save herself. She clambered up into the nearest tree.

All at once the bear let go of Trevor and headed for Patricia. It hit the tree three times

Bear
FACT

Although most bear attacks occur in the wild, it is important to remember that bears in zoos and circuses can also be very dangerous! In 2004, a Russian newspaper reported that when a visitor to a zoo tried to feed a brown bear crackers through the bars of its cage, it bit his hands off. In 1997, a circus bear bit off a small child's finger in Ohio.

In 2005, people were amazed to see a video on television that showed a panda bear at a zoo grabbing a full-grown man who was walking by its cage. The panda pulled the man by his coat and nearly got him into the cage. A zookeeper at the National Zoo in Washington, D.C., was once attacked by Ling-Ling, one of the first pandas displayed in the United States.

It is very important to remember that even animals that look cute and cuddly can be very dangerous.

and stretched to its full height. It used its claws to pull her down. Patricia hit the ground hard.

As scared as she was, she remembered that some park rangers say to play dead in case of a

The bear stretched to its full height. It used its claws to pull Patricia down from the tree.

bear attack. Usually this convinces the bear that you are not a threat. So Patricia rolled up into a ball. But it did no good. She remembers, "I was...on the ground with this bear on top of me chewing on the side of my head." One bite crushed part of her skull.

Patricia was desperate. Being brave, she decided to try to distract the bear and reached out to pinch its nose! Bear biologists recommend that when all else fails, people who are attacked should fight back. In this case, it worked. The bear let go of Patricia and walked away.

Both Trevor and Patricia were seriously wounded, covered in blood. In just a few minutes, two other hikers appeared on the trail. The hikers helped the couple to their feet. They wrapped Patricia's head in a sleeping bag. Slowly, the group walked the three or four miles back to the ranger station.

Park rangers called for help. An ambulance rushed Patricia and Trevor to the hospital for surgery. Trevor needed a complicated operation to rebuild his nose and jaw. Still, his surgery was simple compared to Patricia's. Her entire face had been torn open. Her left eye had been crushed and could not be saved. A huge piece of skin had been torn off the back of her head.

There was no way her injuries could be fixed with just one operation. In fact, she would need thirty. Even after all those operations, she remained terribly scarred.

Following the attack, Trevor soon felt happy. As he put it: "[Isn't] it great to be alive?" He knew there was a good chance he would never be attacked again and felt grateful to have survived.

But Patricia became very depressed. She felt afraid and unable to deal with life. One thing that did help her was writing a book about her experience called *The Bear's Embrace: A True Story of Survival.* Still, she never really got over the attack. In the winter of 2005, she committed suicide.

Bear Encounters

According to bear attack expert Stephen Herrero, people see bears often. Sometimes they see them in the wild—in a national park, for example. From time to time, bears also wander into towns or cities. Still, bears almost never attack humans.

The grizzly that attacked Patricia Van Tighem and Trevor Janz was probably a mother with cubs nearby, like this one.

During most encounters between bears and humans, nothing violent happens. The human and the bear simply look at each other and go off in their own direction.

In Patricia Van Tighem and Trevor Janz's encounter, there were two things that put the couple in danger. First, park rangers figured out that they had encountered a mother bear, probably with cubs nearby. Bears are among the most protective animal mothers on Earth and will fight hard to keep their babies from what they see as harm. Second, the bear was in the middle of a meal. Bears often attack if they are surprised while eating because they do not want other animals to get their food.

Endangered Species

At the turn of the twentieth century, people in the United States and other parts of the world started to work to protect animals and the environment. They were concerned about pollution and began to realize that some of the world's wild animals might soon become extinct.

In 1973, President Richard Nixon signed the Endangered Species Act. It prohibits the hunting of endangered species and protects the habitats in which they live. Other countries also passed their own conservation laws. Today, the World Conservation Union maintains a list of the world's endangered species. "Endangered" species have very few members left and are at great risk of dying out soon. The Union also keeps track of which species are considered "threatened." This means that their population is decreasing fast and the animal might soon become endangered.

The giant panda has been declared an endangered species. The spectacled bear and the sloth bear are listed as threatened. For a long time, the grizzly bear was also considered threatened, but recently its population has started to grow. In November 2005, grizzlies were taken off the threatened list.

A black bear races through a yard in a town in Montana.

Bears are found in many parts of the world, yet most bear attacks seem to happen in North America. This is because of the especially large number of black bears and brown bears that live on the continent. Two hundred years ago, they had vast wilds in which to roam. Today, it seems, humans have built roads and towns all over the land. This has caused the bear population to decrease. At the same time, it has also increased human and bear encounters.

More bear encounters mean more bear attacks. But even though the number of bear attacks has risen, they remain uncommon. On average, bears kill three people a year in North America. They seriously injure between five and fifteen more. Many more people escape a bear attack, having just been scared or hurt slightly.

TWO

Grizzly bears eat both plants and animals and are expert fishers. This one has caught a red salmon.

All About Bears

Humans sometimes describe bears as ferocious man-eaters. At other times, we portray them as cute and cuddly animals. What is the truth? What are bears really like?

One thing many people do not realize is that there are eight species of bear. American black bears are the most common. The other species are the brown bear, polar bear, spectacled bear, Asiatic black bear, sun bear, sloth bear, and panda. The brown bear species includes two subspecies: grizzly bears and Kodiak bears.

One thing that all bears have in common is that their lives revolve around food. Bears are omnivores, meaning that they eat both plants and animals. Scientists consider them opportunistic eaters, which means that rather than searching for favorite foods, they eat whatever they find. This means a brown bear's diet changes from season to season. It feasts on one food while it is plentiful and then, when that food is gone, it looks for something different. For example, at the end of winter, grizzlies eat whatever carrion (dead animals) they can find.

When spring approaches, they eat the nutritious grasses that sprout up. In the summer, they fish for the salmon that appear in the rivers of the West.

Brown bears sometimes track down and kill large animals, such as an elk or moose. (Extremely hungry bears have even been known to stalk humans.) Having stalked its prey, a bear makes a sudden rush at it, using its strong paws to bring the animal down and its long claws and sharp teeth to wound it. Bears bury large kills in a cache, or hiding place, and then sleep nearby, digesting their meal. When they feel hungry again, they dig up the carcass and continue eating it. They will sometimes return

Brown bears use their strong jaws and sharp teeth to wound prey and tear meat. Their back teeth are used for chewing the plants they eat.

to a kill even months later, long after the food has been scavenged by foxes, coyotes, and birds such as ravens, crows, and magpies.

Not all American black bears are black in color. This one is "cinnamon" colored.

Appearance

All bears' bodies are covered with thick fur. Although some species' names seem to indicate their color, this is misleading. For example, all Asiatic black bears are black in color, but not all American black bears are. They can be brown, black, red, cinnamon— even blonde. Brown bears are normally chocolate in color, but can also be almost black or blonde with a brown muzzle (nose) and paws. Polar bears are all white.

Bear species vary widely in terms of size. Sun bears are the smallest species. They are not much bigger than a large dog. By contrast, brown bears can reach heights of ten feet and weigh an average of nine hundred pounds. Polar bears, while they often weigh less than brown bears, grow even taller, up to eleven feet! These facts make it clear why humans are no match for bears in a fight.

Regardless of their species, all bears' bodies look very much alike. Bears are solidly built and

Polar bears are white, which helps them blend in with their snowy and icy surroundings. This camouflage helps them to be better hunters.

carry a lot of weight in their middles. As fall approaches, they put on more and more fat because their bodies must store it for the winter. All bears have short but powerful legs. Overall, bears are very strong animals who are capable of fierce fighting.

Special Features

Bears' bodies are well adapted for their lives of foraging, or searching and hunting for food. Their strong legs easily carry them the long distances they have to travel in order to find enough to eat. Bears usually walk slowly on all four paws, but they can also stand and walk on two legs.

Although people sometimes think bears are clumsy, they can move very quickly. Sometimes bears break into a lope or trot. Running from danger or after prey, they can move as fast as a horse. Black bears are also good at climbing and swimming, although brown bears rarely do.

Bears' paws are very large. Their paws and claws are important tools. With their front paws they

A Bear's Senses

Some scientists say that bears have the best sense of smell of any animal. Bears can detect thousands more smells than humans can. They use their noses to locate mates, identify cubs, avoid humans, and find food. A black bear in California was known to have smelled a dead deer three miles away. Even more amazing, a polar bear smelled a seal from a distance of thirty miles!

Bears probably see about as well as humans do. They have good night vision, which allows them to move about easily in the dark. Even so, bears' sense of sight does not help them find food nearly as much as their sense of smell does. In fact, hunters in Alaska once encountered a blind polar bear that seemed to not be having any trouble finding food at all (they based this judgment on the fact that the bear was fat).

Experts also believe that bears have good hearing. For example, people have noticed that bears can hear a camera shutter click from a distance of fifty feet. Bears use their hearing mostly to avoid danger.

Brown Bear
FACTs

Brown bears are the most dangerous to humans.
Height: Five to eight feet
Weight: 350–850 pounds
Diet: Plants, small animals such as mice,
   larger animals such as deer, and fish
Habitat: Open country in the mountains
Life span: In the wild, fifteen to thirty years

can pick up everything from heavy boulders to tree limbs. Bears are so dexterous, meaning that they have great control over their paws, that they can even open jars of food!

Behavior

Most bears tend to avoid humans, but they are intelligent and learn fast. This means that once they find out that humans at campgrounds, for example, have food they like, they return to look for it. They can learn to recognize food sources like garbage cans and picnic baskets.

In the wild, bears spend much of their lives alone. Bears do not share their territories with other bears. This is because a territory may not have

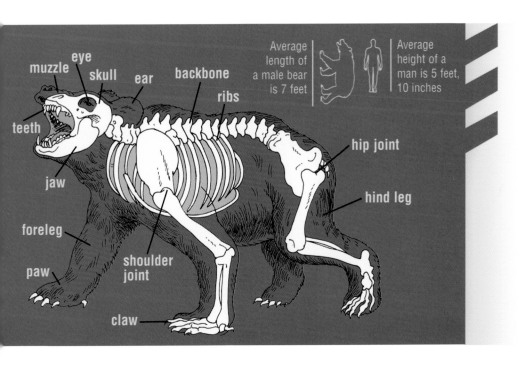

muzzle eye skull ear backbone ribs

teeth

jaw

foreleg

paw shoulder joint

claw

Average length of a male bear is 7 feet

Average height of a man is 5 feet, 10 inches

hip joint

hind leg

enough food for two or more bears. An adult male will mark out his own territory, sometimes urinating on trees to let other bears know by scent that he has taken possession of a piece of land. Female bears, known as sows, also have their own territories, but they are smaller and sometimes overlap with males' territories. A brown bear's territory may be as small as ten square miles or as large as 350 square miles, depending on the land and food available.

Bears are found in groups only where there is a large source of food, such as when a river is full of salmon. Male and female bears also come together for a short while in the summer to mate.

In the warm weather, they are sometimes seen relaxing or playing. In the fall, they spend as much time as possible eating. When winter comes, food becomes very hard to find. Some bears hibernate, going to sleep until the cold passes.

When winter comes, bears need dens in which to hibernate and take shelter. Dens differ widely from species to species. American black bears may use small caves or burrow under tree roots. Brown bears usually dig holes in which to sleep. Other times, they use a cave or a hollow tree. Polar bears tunnel into snow.

When some mammals, such as woodchucks, hibernate, their heart rate becomes extremely slow

Where Do Bears Live?

American black bears: Most parts of the United States and parts of Mexico.

Brown bears: North America, Europe, and Asia.

Asiatic black bears: Asia

Polar bears: The Arctic Circle, Alaska, northern Canada, Russia, and Norway.

Spectacled bears: The Andes Mountains of South America. They are the only bears that live south of the equator.

Sloth bears: India

Pandas: China

Sun bears: Malaysia

A three-month-old polar bear cub emerges from its den. Bears are born in the winter, during hibernation.

and their body temperature falls to almost freezing. Bear hibernation is different. Instead of a deep sleep, bears spend many days dozing. If disturbed, they will wake up right away. Their body temperature does not drop as drastically, and their heart rate remains almost normal.

Female bears give birth while in hibernation. Bear cubs are born tiny—about the size of puppies— and naked. Mothers stay in their dens nursing their babies for four or five months. They leave the den only when warm weather comes. By this time, the cubs are bigger and strong enough to walk along with their mother. She teaches them to look for food, and they eat the green leaves and buds she shows them. Cubs stay with their mother for two to three years. This gives them plenty of time to learn to hunt and fish.

Three

Bears are opportunistic eaters, which means they will eat
whatever is available. This includes any food humans throw away.

Hungry Bears

Imagine waking from a sound sleep to find yourself under attack by a bear. That is what happened one night in July 2003 in Rocky Mountain National Park, in Colorado. Visitors to the park marvel at its eagles, hawks, elk, mule deer, moose, bighorn sheep, coyotes, and cougars. It is also very exciting to see the many black bears in the park. Of course, no one wants to see them up close.

Five friends were camping at a site near Fern Lake. Settling in, they cooked dinner. Afterward, they relaxed by the fire. By the time they were ready for bed, they had hung all their food from the "bear pole" the park provided for campers. Many national parks provide these poles, which have wires or hooks mounted very high, to hang food out of the reach of bears. Bears can smell the food, but they quickly learn that they cannot get to it. This discourages them and they usually move on.

Patrick Finan was sound asleep when suddenly a black bear bit through his tent's lining, going right for his head. "It was a blur," Finan said later. He struggled to get to his feet and ran out of the tent, shouting and yelling. Blood gushed from his head, but he could see that the bear—which he estimated weighed about 250 pounds—was moving on to another tent, about thirty yards away. It then tried to get into that tent. But after one swipe at the head of Tim Schuett, who was sleeping inside, the bear lumbered away.

By this time, all of the campers were awake. Terrified, they used a cell phone to notify park rangers of what had happened. The rangers called an ambulance and Finan and Schuett

How to Teach Bears

After a bear attacks a person in a national park, rangers hunt down the attacker. Sometimes they believe they have no choice but to kill the bear so it will not harm anyone else. However, rangers want to avoid doing this, if possible. They try to prevent attacks by controlling bears. One method park rangers use to control bears is aversive conditioning.

In aversive conditioning, a bear is permitted to enter a "human zone" such as a picnic site or campground. When it does, park rangers do something unpleasant to the bear. They might shoot it with rubber bullets, for example, or let dogs chase it. As soon as the bear begins to run away, the "punishment" stops. Eventually, in order to avoid "punishment," the bear learns to avoid these human zones.

were taken to a hospital, where their head wounds were checked out. They soon left the hospital, and both recovered a short time later.

In the meantime, park rangers searched for the bear. An hour after the attack, another camper across the lake videotaped what was probably the same bear trying to break open a locked food-storage container. Park rangers hoped they would be able to catch the bear in a trap, but they did not succeed.

In a demonstration at a wildlife refuge in California, a black bear destroys a standard plastic cooler to get at a small amount of honey.

Two weeks later, hikers told a park ranger they had seen the bear and that it was acting very aggressively. When the park ranger found the bear, it began to circle him. Fearing for his life, the ranger shot and killed it. As Rocky Mountain National Park superintendent, Vaughn Baker, told reporters, rangers kill bears only in extreme situations. He said this bear seemed to have learned to associate people with food and was thus extremely dangerous.

Historic Encounters

Bear attacks are nothing new. In 1691, a European explorer named Henry Kelsey wrote a poem about the grizzlies he saw in Manitoba, Canada. He described them as the animal that "makes food of man."

Two hundred years ago, Meriwether Lewis and William Clark, the first American explorers to cross the North American continent and reach the Pacific Ocean, noted that the Native Americans they met on their trip were clearly and understandably wary of bears. Even though the Native Americans regularly hunted bears, they recognized their danger. It seems every tribe Lewis and Clark encountered had stories to tell of bears that had attacked hunting parties.

Keeping Park Visitors Safe

Bears once roamed the wilderness all over North America. Today, outside of the wilds of Alaska and northern Canada, grizzly bears are largely confined to a few national parks. Black bears live in the wild almost everywhere in the continental United States. Bears are one of the things that draw visitors to national parks, including Banff National Park in Canada, and Yosemite, Yellowstone, and Glacier National Parks in the United States. At parks with bears, rangers spend a lot of time and effort keeping visitors safe from bear attacks. For the most part, they succeed.

WARNING!

The future of bears and the safety of others depends on you.

Day Users: Food and Odors Attract Bears

ALL food, beverages, cooking equipment, pet food, and garbage MUST be in your immediate control at all times. Garbage must also be packed out. Please do not place garbage or food scraps in the fire rings. Thank you for your cooperation.

Grand Island National Recreation Area
Hiawatha National Forest

In the 1960s, national park rangers realized that bears were feeding from the parks' trash cans and garbage dumps. Parks did away with this problem by getting rid of the dumps. Rangers also taught campers and hikers to store trash in their cars or in special bear-proof containers. Still, park bears have learned over time that humans carry food. This is one reason that attacks do sometimes occur. In Yellowstone, there were a total of thirty-two attacks that resulted in injury between 1980 and 2002.

Four

In Manitoba, Canada, a polar bear inspects a tourist bus. Each year many tourists go to see these dangerous predators.

Danger: Polar Bears!

For thousands of years, Inuit, the native people who live along the Arctic Ocean in the wilderness of Alaska and far northern Canada, have spent the summers fishing and hunting, stocking up on the food they will need to get through the long dark winters.

In July 1999, a large Inuit family and some friends left their village in Nunavut territory to camp, fish, and hunt on Corbett Inlet. They expected this to be a good time, during which the family's elders could teach their grandchildren the skills their own grandparents had taught them.

However, tragedy struck the camp. One afternoon, sixty-six-year-old Moses Aliyak and his twelve-year-old grandson Cyrus looked out of their tent to see that their boat was adrift. They set right out to retrieve it. At first, everything was fine. Then, out of nowhere, there appeared a polar bear. It stood six feet tall and, at 250 or 300 pounds, far outweighed the man and the boy.

Moses tried to scare the bear away by throwing rocks and yelling, making as much noise as

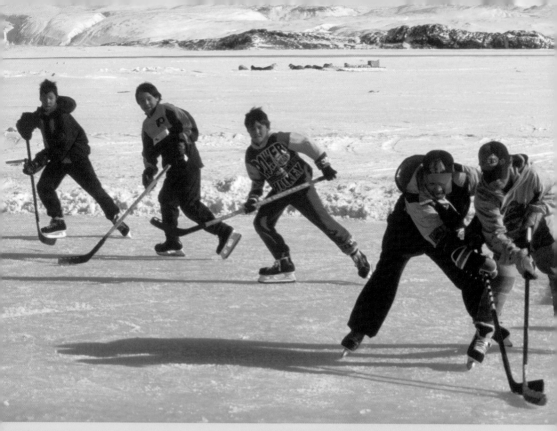

Along with hunting and fishing, ice hockey is an activity enjoyed by many in Nunavut Territory. But any outdoor activity must be enjoyed with caution because of the region's polar bears.

he could. But the polar bear showed no fear. Instead, it came at him. The bear slashed Moses's head and face with its huge paws. Moses could not get away.

Terrified, Cyrus ran back and hid in the tent. It was then that other campers, Hattie Amnitak and her ten-year-old grandson Eddie, realized that something horrible was happening. They went to help Moses. The huge animal then turned on Hattie, batting her about with its paws and biting her. The bear also struck Eddie, landing a severe blow to his head.

Still another camper, Margaret Amarook, had gone off to get water at a nearby spring. She was expecting someone to come soon to help her. When no one arrived, she went back to the campsite to see what was going on. Imagine her shock when she found both Moses and Eddie lying on the ground, covered in blood. Hattie was dead. By now the bear was gone, so Margaret could only guess what had happened.

Although Moses was in a great deal of pain, he and Margaret quickly decided that she should try to make it to another nearby camp for help. Hurriedly,

The bear slashed Moses's head and face with its huge paws. Moses could not get away.

she took off on foot, racing to the camp of another family. There she used a shortwave radio to call for help. Helicopters brought wildlife officers and trauma nurses to the camp.

Later, wildlife officers went back to the scene, tracked the bear, killed it, and took its body away to be examined. There was never a news report saying what the examination revealed, but other studies show that polar bears are seldom seen so far south in Nunavut at that time of year. This bear might have been sick or starving, and in search of food.

Polar Bear Folklore

Polar bears were often the subject of many Inuit myths and stories. In one story, Nanuk, the master of bears, was chased by a pack of dogs. The chase went on for hours upon hours until suddenly the animals reached the end of Earth. There they leapt into the sky, where they became the stars.

Inuit also told stories of mythical bear-men, polar bears who lived in igloos. When they reached home, they would remove their fur.

Inuit so respected polar bears that they treated their dead bodies very carefully. Hunters hung the skins of bears they killed inside their igloos. In front of them, they would place tools. They believed the bears took the tools' "power" into the afterlife.

Seal is what polar bears eat most often because it is the most plentiful meat in their frozen habitat.

Polar Bear Dangers

Polar bears live farther north than any other land mammal except the arctic fox. Most of the year polar bears are on the move, searching for food. On land they eat any plants they can find. But since plants are hard to find in frozen climates, polar bears are mostly carnivores, or meat-eaters. Their hunt for food also takes them off the land and far out onto the very thick ice that surrounds the North Pole. There they hunt for their favorite food: seal. Using their massive strength, they also kill walrus and—if they are very, very lucky—beluga whales. Females with new cubs spend winters hibernating in caves they dig in the snow. Males remain on the ice.

Until the 1800s, white men of North America and Europe knew nothing of polar bears. They simply had never traveled to where polar bears live. Settlements would eventually spread into Alaska and northern Canada. Today, tourists go to the frozen north especially to see polar bears.

Even though human and polar bear encounters have become more frequent in the past one hundred years, polar bear attacks remain rare. But even though polar bears seldom attack humans, they should be seen as extremely dangerous. One of the largest predators on Earth, they are very powerful and can be quite aggressive. People who

In search of food, polar bears sometimes venture into towns, where they pose more of a threat to humans. These polar bears explore a yard in Manitoba, Canada.

go into polar bear territory are warned to take precautions. For example, visitors to the territory of Svarbard, in Norway, are told to carry guns whenever they go beyond the outskirts of a town.

One thing that worries experts is that more and more polar bears have been sighted in or near towns. In 2003, for example, sixty bears appeared on a beach near Barrow, Alaska. They had come to feast on whale carcasses. Town officials closed the road that went to the beach to prevent people from going out to see the bears.

Once the meat ran out, the bears started to go into the town. They looked for food around houses

Polar bears are extremely dangerous. They are very powerful and can be quite aggressive.

and in Dumpsters. When officials came across polar bears, they scared them away with firecrackers. One bear had to be killed because it kept returning.

Experts worry about bears in towns for two reasons. First, they want to prevent people from being attacked. Second, they do not want to have to kill bears, even if they are a danger to people.

Five

American black bears are expert tree climbers. But it is
extremely rare for a grizzly, like this one, to climb a tree.

Too Close

Al Johnson was a game biologist for the state of Alaska. He helped the government track and identify big animals such as bears and wolves. One September day in 1973, he went to Mount McKinley (now Denali) National Park to photograph the moose who lived there.

Inside the park, he sighted a sow grizzly and three cubs, peacefully grazing on green plants. For several hours, Johnson followed the bears, photographing them from a safe distance. Not wanting to alert the bears to his presence, he never got close to them. The bears showed no sign that they knew Johnson was there.

By the end of the afternoon, Johnson had taken many photographs, but he still wanted more. He decided to try to get a few last good close-ups. To do so, he climbed up into what he believed was a safe and sturdy tree.

To lure the bears closer Johnson made squeaking sounds like a rabbit. The cubs heard him and came over right away, while their mother went on looking for food. Johnson kept squeaking, trying to get her attention as well. Finally, the mother bear came bounding toward the tree to investigate.

Johnson realized he was in danger, but he wanted more photos. He began to focus his camera on the cubs. He said to himself, "What a fantastic photo this will be!" Then, suddenly, one of the cubs let out a cry.

In response, the mother bear used her strength to shake the tree violently. Next, she seemed to run right up the tree. Using her claws, she got hold of Johnson's boot and pulled him to the ground.

Once on the ground, Johnson covered his face with his arms. One, two, three, four times, she bit each of his arms. With her huge paws, she clawed his head. Then her mouth closed on his shoulder. She lifted him off the ground and then dropped him. Johnson rolled onto his stomach and used his hands to try to protect the back of his neck. The bear tried to bite the small of his back. Then, she got his head in her mouth.

Later, Johnson said he did not remember feeling any pain. But he was terrified because he thought he could hear his skull being crushed.

Finally, the bear and her cubs departed. Johnson has never figured out exactly why the mother bear stopped attacking him. "She evidently figured I wouldn't give her any more problems," he said in an interview. When Johnson knew the bears were gone, he got up and started to walk toward the road. He could hardly see. One eye was swollen shut and the other would barely open.

The road was only two or three hundred steps away, but Johnson was so badly hurt that he had to lie down twice to rest. Less than a minute after he finally made it to the road, two vehicles appeared. Their drivers stopped and got him help. He was airlifted to a hospital. "I was a bloody mess," he remembered.

In the operating room, doctors used skin from his leg to close up the largest wound on his head.

A mother brown bear stands to look out for any dangers that might threaten her three cubs.

Why Do Bears Attack?

"Killer Grizzly Strikes Again." "Bear Mauls and Kills Infant." "Camper Leaps off Cliff to Escape Bear Attack." Newspapers that report bear attacks often include grisly details but they do not always answer one basic question: Why do bears attack?

Bears do not attack because they are mean. They do not always attack because they want to eat people. They may attack because they, or their cubs, are being threatened.

A bear may also attack because it is desperately hungry. The bear may have gotten lost and cannot find enough food. Sometimes the food it is used to eating is no longer available. For example, a long dry spell with no rain can mean there is no berry crop, or the construction of a new housing development can mean that the animals bears usually eat have fled the area.

Very old or sick bears also have trouble finding enough to eat. Hunger can drive such bears to attack.

One of his arteries had been torn and had to be patched back together.

During his recovery, Johnson had plenty of time to think about what had happened. He realized that he never should have tried to get close to the bears. Mount McKinley park rangers decided that the bear had been provoked and would not otherwise be dangerous. They did not look for the bear family.

Provoked Attacks

At times, bear attacks happen due to no fault of the person involved. A park ranger, for example, may surprise a mother bear with her cubs, or a hiker may come across a bear feeding on a carcass. A camper may follow all of a park's rules, including putting food in an airtight container, and still have a bear come sniffing around. Experts use the word "unprovoked" to describe this kind of attack.

Other attacks are considered "provoked." This means that the victim did something to cause the bear to attack. Perhaps a dog accompanying a hiker rushed at a bear, barking at and threatening it. Or, a wildlife photographer, like Al Johnson, might have gotten too close.

These cases teach one very important lesson: bears attack when they perceive a threat to themselves, their young, or their food. Humans must make every effort not to make bears feel threatened. This is the best way to avoid bear attacks.

SIX

Human and bear encounters are increasing. If you go to bear country, it is good to keep some safety tips in mind.

Help!

Probably the foremost authority in the world on bear attacks today is Dr. Stephen Herrero. In June 1967, Dr. Herrero graduated with a Ph.D. in animal behavior from the University of California at Berkeley. That summer the news broke that two women had been killed in Glacier National Park in Montana by two different grizzly bears. The news sparked Herrero's interest in bear attacks, and he began to study them.

Herrero has since gathered a vast amount of data about bear attacks. National parks call him in after bear attacks to help figure out what happened. He also helps parks decide where to locate new hiking trails and campgrounds to avoid as many human and bear encounters as possible. With his knowledge of bear behavior, Herrero knows where bears are most likely to visit and offers advice on how to avoid bear attacks.

Bear attacks are truly horrifying, but they occur very rarely and can often be avoided. If you are among the many people who love the wilderness and would like to observe bears in their natural habitat, do plan a trip to one of North America's national parks. Just remember that it is important to respect bears, just as it is to protect nature.

How to Avoid
a Bear Attack

Based on information from bear attack experts, the Canadian National Park Service offers advice to campers and hikers on how to avoid a bear attack. They say:

1. Make noise. Singing, talking, or wearing bells while hiking warns bears that you are in the area.

2. Keep all dogs on leashes so they do not run at and startle a bear.

3. Watch for signs that bears might be nearby. Signs include bear droppings, and trees that have been stripped of bark, clawed, or bitten. Big tracks with long claws are a sign that bears have been in the area. If you see any of these signs, leave the area at once.

4. Stay on marked trails so you do not become lost (and can be found easily if there is an attack).

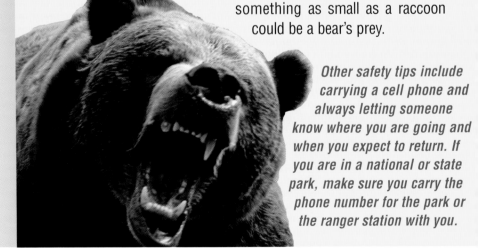

5. Never approach a dead animal. Even something as small as a raccoon could be a bear's prey.

Other safety tips include carrying a cell phone and always letting someone know where you are going and when you expect to return. If you are in a national or state park, make sure you carry the phone number for the park or the ranger station with you.

What to Do If
You Are Attacked

Because people do encounter bears in the wild from time to time, national parks also offer advice as to what to do in that case:

1. Stay calm. Sudden noise or movement can trigger an attack.

2. Do not run from a bear. (This does not hold true at night or if you are being stalked by a bear. In those cases, it is best to try to escape.)

3. Speak quietly. Some experts say this will help a bear recognize that you are not a threat.

4. If you are in a group, stay together. It is important to leave a bear an escape route. In other words, do not surround a bear!

5. If a bear approaches you, use bear spray, aiming at the animal's face. Bear spray is made from the oils of hot peppers. It will sting a bear's eyes and nose.

6. If bear spray does not make the bear go away, play dead, lying facedown on the ground. Spread your legs apart. Lace your fingers and use your hands to protect the back of your head and your neck. The bear may conclude that you are dead and cannot hurt it.

7. If the bear still continues its attack, fight back.

Glossary

aversive conditioning—A method that teaches a bear to avoid human zones by "punishing" it when it approaches those zones.

cache—A hidden area where a bear stores its food.

carcass—The body of a dead animal.

den—A place where a bear or other wild animal sleeps.

encounter—A meeting or interaction.

endangered—Close to being extinct.

habitat—The area in which an animal lives. A suitable habitat includes enough water, food, space, and shelter.

hibernate—To spend the winter asleep to conserve energy and survive.

omnivore—An animal that eats both plants and meat.

polar ice—The huge pack of ice formed from seawater in the central Arctic Ocean.

predator—An animal that hunts other animals for food.

prey—An animal that is hunted for food.

sow—An adult female bear.

species—A group of similar animals. Members of a species look similar to one another and can mate and produce offspring.

territory—An animal's home area, which it will often defend.

Books

Becker, John E. *Grizzly Bears.* Mankato, Minn.: KidHaven Press, 2003.

Herrero, Stephen. *Bear Attacks: Their Causes and Avoidance.* Guilford, Conn.: Lyons Press, 2002.

Hirschi, Ron. *Searching for Grizzlies.* Honesdale, Pa.: Boyds Mills Press, 2005.

Miller, Debbie S. *A Polar Bear Journey.* New York: Walker & Company, 2005.

Montgomery, Sy. *Search for the Golden Moon Bear.* New York: Houghton Mifflin, 2004.

Smithsonian Handbook of Mammals. New York: Dorling Kindersley, 2002.

Swinburne, Stephen R. *Black Bear: North America's Bear.* Honesdale, Pa.: Boyds Mills Press, 2003.

Internet Addresses

North Cascades National Park: Bear Country
<http://www.nps.gov/noca/bear.htm>

Polar Bears @ nationalgeographic.com
<http://www.nationalgeographic.com/ngm/0012/feature2/>

WildCam: Brown Bears @ nationalgeographic.com
<http://www.nationalgeographic.com/bearcam/gallery/index.html>

Index